dragonflies

For Jane

Crumps Barn Studio
Syde, Cheltenham GL53 9PN
www.crumpsbarnstudio.co.uk

Cover design by Lorna Gray

Typeset in Adobe Garamond Pro

All our books are printed on responsibly sourced paper from managed woodlands
and recycled material. Printed in the UK by TJ Books, Padstow.

ISBN 978-1-915067-53-1

dragonflies

Graham Powell

Crumps Barn Studio

AND FOUND

They say that in the end we're reunited
With all we've lost – not love and circumstance
But umbrellas, tissues and socks
Or, in my case, that one photograph
Tucked inside the book wedged halfway down –
Or was it up – the bookshelf we once had
Shortly before we moved or stayed –
I can't remember which – but the photo
Is lost somewhere between *Ulysses* and
The biography of a little-known hedonist.

And maybe now I've forgotten the photo too:
Was I, for example, on your left or
Right arm and were you smiling or merely
Squinting a direction at the lens –
Who knows? Well, someday someone will
When the lot is sold, and you are found
Tucked between the pages that I left
Unread that day – or was it night – many years ago.

GLASS

There is an extended moment in falling
When we can do no more than watch and wait
For the eventual crash that brings us back
To where we were before; to find all's changed
And nothing can be made that's whole again.

So it was for you as the glass spun
Out of your control and splashed in pieces
Never to regain the shape it once held
Those hundred years ago, and you knew well
What was lost and couldn't be remade.

Not, of course, the thing itself but what tied
Us to it in this place and at that time;
The evening was broken for you now
With nothing left to ease you back to where
You were those fragile moments just before.

But – out of reach – there was that other loss
Of something spinning helplessly in space
That never would regain itself again
And you could see it passing through the air
To end undone as insubstantial as a sigh.

MISE EN SCÈNE

We always knew there was something missing –
That we'd come this far only to leave
The question hanging in the back of our minds,
Lodged like a dead bat in the attic –
Still warm and waiting for us to return
At some point in the future that we knew
Would never come no matter what we had said,
What promises we'd made to ourselves,
When we'd looked around for one last time
Before turning out the light and closing fast the door.

Since when, it's all felt incomplete
As if we'd left at the interval
And still didn't know how it turned out for them
Or even if there was some resolution
To make it all worthwhile after all
The entrances and exits had happened off stage
While we were, as we have been, elsewhere
Awaiting our passage to the other place
That was being organised for us
All along despite our ignorance.

Maybe we comply too easily
And don't open up old wounds as much as we should
When the telephone rings or the letter lies –
As it used to do – unopened on the mat
Waiting for a reply or some response
That shows that whatever it was that's missing
Is still within our range and scope
Even though we know we'd sooner forget
And just – as they say – move on, leave it behind,
Allow the hole to fill itself in time.

PARALLAX

Totally foxed after years in transit
And simply just waiting to be read
The Bernard Patrick Prize for Geography
Has for the last six weeks been off the shelf.

The glue along the spine has finally cracked,
The front cover's breaking free, misaligned
And fraying at the corners it may not last
Until I've reached the final page.

In 1969, newly published,
It was the book I simply had to have;
Stately, plump, uncompromisingly black,
James Joyce's *Ulysses* – in spectrum white font –

Has travelled with me to study bedrooms
Through marriages and shelves beneath the stairs,
Viewed by children who, unimpressed, left it
As I did – regularly – until another day;

Twenty pages and then I'd stall again
And let more dampness seep into the grain
To swell each page and turn them soft and brown;
Smelling of ripeness and readiness

For forty years until I prised
It from the tight packed shelf and let it spin.
It's spinning still and I'm getting there at last;
These ruminations on a single day,

Whose time has come to pass, is making me
See things that I thought far away, come closer
Day by day – like rings on middle fingers
And furtive, slinking dogs – decoded and

Unearthed – and like the book itself – just waiting
To be noticed, re-examined, held up
For closer scrutiny, spilling their matters
Ineluctable onto an empty page.

WAITING GAME

As things turned out, they'd been there all along
Exchanging knowing looks and tiresome sighs:
Beyond impatience, merely trapped
Within the compass of my gaze but out of sight,
Willing to reappear when needed or,
If not, to play another hand of whist,
Or tumble dice or light a cigarette.

Ready either way – made up with fake tan
And a handful of complimentary tickets –
Quite indifferent, it seemed, about the outcome
Until I cleared my throat and saw them packing up:
Rearranging the cushions and the rugs,
Straightening the tables and the backless chairs,
Timed out and heading home again.

AT BAY

Plucked in summer from the bush, it's dry now
Hung from a hook all winter it's as crisp
As any dead thing, free of taste or smell,
Honed knife-sharp with edges ready soon to crack
With all the dryness of a life that's spent.

Until, that is, I float it in a pan that's warm
With water brought slowly to the boil
On which it sits – half-submerged and turning –
Feeling again the heat upon its back,
Those warm and tender fingers unloosening the knot.

I place my eyes level with the water's edge
And watch it as it spins – growing greener now –
With veins that – slackening – expand and glow
Releasing all that's left, seeping from inside:
The sweet yet pungent savour of regret.

SPRING CLEANING

This is the end of winter
And the great clearance is at hand:
You wash finger dabs from the cupboards
While I pull fistfuls of stuff from behind drawers.

Stuff that has fallen silently all winter
As we were going about our busy business –
Pegs, wine bags, dishcloths and greaseproof paper –
Until the drawer would shut no more.

And now we discover a nest of spoons
We never knew we had, until now,
That has arrived piecemeal in our lives
From picnics, train trips and other people's homes.

So much gradual accumulation
That we must clear before it's all too late
And we subside beneath the tide, drowning
In the flood of jetsam we have made.

I wash my yellowed toenails from the bath,
And walk – naked in socks – into the room
Where you are rousing from a night of soapy dreams
Ready to cast adrift and start again.

ESTATE AGENT

We're looking through a window
At someone else's life
Lived in the space that once we knew
Twenty-five years ago.

Rearranging their furniture:
We push their bed against the other wall
And place that chair we used to have
Beneath the window where it was.

The shape cannot have changed
But all that was within has come and gone
And all those things we might have done
Are stacked up in their attic biding time.

We think we could return
Roll back the years – now that it's just we two –
Discard the trappings of the life we've lived
And slip back snugly into what we were.

We know it can't be done
That going back is really giving up
That nothing that was – past – can be reclaimed
And nothing's really all that would be found

Apart that is from the slap of your feet
On the basement steps those mornings before work
And the pictures tacked and curled upon the wall
Of daffodils, Miles Davis and the sea

All gone, gathered and discarded when we left
Moving on to something better,
Replaced by what some others would put there
In making sense of what makes up their lives

While we were making other sense of ours
Never knowing that we'd see it all again
Partially distorted by the window's glass
In someone else's half-occluded life.

AQUILEGIA

Unto and of itself
arriving unbidden
self-seeded – broadcasting

its seeds haphazardly –
forgetful, unintended
just leaving things to chance

they gather in ones and twos
ill-disposed to measured plots
inclined to cracks and gaps

between the orderly
the crafted and contrived
surprised themselves by where

they have appeared –
altered but essentially
the same in shape and leaf

holding their own against
the broken earth until
they trust themselves to throw

a shoot into the air
fresh-leafed and furred in bud
eager to inspect

head bowed and undisclosed
then gradually
revealing flutes and furls

the trumpets of the high
baroque though disinclined
to make a fuss or fret

they turn again to seed
unheralded in pods
of seamed and polished green

that dry to husks that split
and spill themselves unseen
and fall

careless and remote
content to be re-cast
remodelled and reshaped

into some other self
though unaware quite when
or where or whether that will be

LOCHAN LUNN DA BHRA

The cuckoo is changing his tune:
All day and half into the night
We've heard him and once,
With tail cocked on a fence post,
I saw him as the light closed in –
Insistent and incessantly
Hammering at the rocks until

We'd had enough and had to free ourselves
From all this hemming in;
We walked out on the moors and climbed
Until the loch came into view
And massive granite shoulders hunched and bunched
Beneath a sky of clouds turned pink
And full as heather or as yellow and

As steadfast and true as bog asphodel
Clinging to the peat and drowning
In the mazy purl of waters – confounding
Us until a dark brown scar
Appeared that wove its jagged thread
Deep into the turf and deeper to the loch –
As flat and bright as zinc as night appeared.

By dawn a wind is ruffling leaves
And making the stands of grass move
In circles all about themselves.
Sun catches on the tops and cuts
Dark clefts into a hill that's drifting
Away then coming closer all the time.
The wind drops and lands everything

In its right place and in its right mind:
The sheep are so disposed to bleat again
On a hillside that's warming to the sun.
And soon we'll take our place amongst it all:
Picking out paths and cutting corners until
The cuckoo starts its stitching round the byre
With upturned notes that hem us in again.

ARBORETUM

Nothing much has changed, apart from the trees
That have, as you might expect, grown bigger
Just as we have, being older now than you

Were when, remember, you placed those shoes
On the roof of the car just before we
Drove away and how – unnoticed – they fell

Never to be recovered unless of course,
Like all those other things we lost, you have them now
Along with the imagined memories

Of the grandchildren that you never knew
And the conversations we might have had
While you were waiting for something to happen

Glancing at your watch and noticing that
The hands had ceased to move and were set
Just as they had been the last time that you checked.

Meanwhile we have been letting the days run down
Until we've nothing left to do
But wonder if we might have arrived just too late

And found that, despite it all, you've gone
To leave us stranded here at the terminal lounge
With nothing but the tick of the stationary clock

And a nagging sense that we've forgotten something
Though as yet we're quite uncertain of what
It is that we have left so very far behind

PAPERCLIP

Falls unbid – late morning approaching noon –
Clatters from a hem or pocket onto
The bedroom chair whereon it skids and sits

And poses questions of its provenance:
The ticket stubs it clipped, the notes it held
Together, currency or photographs,

Receipts for things we bought that later we
Consigned in drawers or half-way down a pile
Of papers that we thought we might just need sometime.

I wonder why it has resurfaced here
And why – like words upon a page – it has
Set my mind adrift again to ponder

Just where anything goes – like handkerchiefs
And love – as ubiquitous as the dead
And as unsought for as those moments when

They rise to greet us – like paperclips or tea –
Always welcome and maybe of some use
Though – like as not – to be consigned into

The box we've left unmarked as *Just too difficult*
Or that other one we keep for useful
Odds and bits that in the end we know we'll

Never use, just like a poem that's half left
And hanging like a question mark – trying
To turn an answer into a neat full stop.

LATE MORNING

Turning, thinking she had heard a sentence
Recognisable of a life though not
Her own, she saw, in the reflection of
What she thought had been unsaid, all those things
That she had experienced in the past.

It passed until she, looking again, cleared
Her throat as if to ask them if she had
Been mistaken previously or if
They had, like herself, remembered how it
Felt to be betrayed or, at least, deceived.

But they had finished, turned the page and left
The unfinished business for another day
When, uninhibited by the company
Of strangers, they might, resharpen their edges
And resume, from where they had left off, without her.

Which left her in an uncomfortable
Position; blithely unaware of the
Truth of their situation but forced painfully
To confront all the things they'd left unsaid
In her own impervious relationship.

She would, she said, confront him – have it out –
Just as those others had or so she thought
Having only heard the very tip of
What they had been saying, over coffee,
At the table from which his back was turned.

KINETON SONNETS

1

Even today when the sharp tang of box
Hit the back of my throat at Miserden
I could hear the knocker's dull thud and then
The patient wait for the door to be unlocked:
Peg, I'll have you, will you be quiet now.
The dog's yap and its scratchy claws sliding
On the frayed lino – with her voice chiding –
Snuffling at the draught crack like an old sow.
And once inside, of course, there's no one there:
No one in the cold front room that's kept for best
Nothing stuck fast to the dry flypaper
That's hanging from the beam and turning in the air.
These dead echoes coming from nowhere.
Framed photos someplace else and lost.

2

So many entrances and exits
In the cupboards of the polished range:
Doors flying open and closed on hinges
That creaked and banged and brought forth brisket
Bacon, egg custards, fruit scones, bread and pies –
Like watching the magician's assistant
Sawn in two then brought back again –
I blinked at the marvel before my eyes.
The miracle and husbandry of fires
That warmed and cleansed and aired the lives of men
Was passed down to our forebears at their birth
Made holy in this simple votive hearth
And the certain semaphore of doors.
Raked embers in a copper warming pan.

3

The larder door was heavy and the latch
Beyond reach – all the better to seal
The tomb of cold, damp air inside and keep
The stone slabs moist and chill to the touch.
A pile of potatoes – musty in sacks –
The husky smell of chicken meal and corn
Hanging in the shadows of the gabardine
Mac that clung in pleats from a nail at the back.
They'd send me there to get some cheese or bread
Netted or stacked further back beyond
The plate of sprats, butter in a glass bowl,
Further back, away from mice or, as I feared,
Rats. If asked to go there on my own –
I shook the latch, banged the door and held my breath.

4

Your breath came thickly through the long dark night
As I lay there watching the net on your head,
And your mouth go toothless slack then gum tight –
Toothless slack then gum tight – and he was dead –
Three months dead – and you being frightened by death
Had me stay by you for company's sake
In case – at night – you too should lose your breath
And all those ritual promises would break.
I watched the pictures on the wall till dawn:
Victoria and Daniel in the Lion's Den
Staring unblinking with those eyes of doom
That scanned and judged each corner of the room –
Myself included hunched up in the bed
Surrounded by your snores and all the dead.

5

He's catching flies again – just let him rest –
The man I'm learning fast to be myself,
Sixty years on – his head upon his chest,
Bone weary, his teeth placed on the shelf.
Beneath the tock of the afternoon clock,
His head lurches forward and then snaps back
Hearing the murmur of distant voices
In the hum of the wireless hanging in the air.
Three o'clock: the tea skins and grows cold,
The newspaper falls from his knee and folds
Itself neatly at his feet; completely
Unaware his fingers fumble mutely
Trying to grab hold of something that was there
Slipping fast away into the thin air.

6

The major sent his laundry to be washed
On Mondays in an old brown case
Tied across its width with a tight cord string
That kept the lid intact because the hinge
Was shot – its campaign days long over
Now called up for this domestic service:
The weekly container for slightly soiled
Clothes and hems in need of some modest repair.
Always rather gentle and abashed
By this unwonted tenderness
He would avert his eyes – and so would you –
Both made awkward, clumsy and wordless
By such near intimacy of the flesh,
Unsure – after the wash – what to say or do.

And it all depends on that squat brass tap
Stiff as a tightly locked stopcock
Strapped to the pipe on the distempered wall
Hissing and spurting a full fat shock
Into the plugless sink of chipped brown tiles
Leaving you breathless gasping, grasping at
The towel – blinded by the sharp pink soap –
That rolled from the rail at the back of the door.
Stripped down to your vest you'd *have a swill,*
Spray the floor with spluttery spume,
Corkscrew your ears with that rough-dry towel
And, with hair pomaded – slicked flat – hope
That – catching your eye in the mirrored glass –
You'd find some girl, have a chat and make a pass.

8

We were naughty boys weren't we? you said,
Seeking my approval for a life lived
Other than how you always had me live
Since I was your son and always would *behave.*
London boys they were, from the East End
Cocky – thought they knew it all and we were
Country bumpkins – we showed them in the end
Who would be cock of the walk round here.
So, two brothers gathered summer holly,
Slipped it – upstairs – in between the sheets
And waited breath-bated for those prickled screams
Followed – soon after – by their father fiercely
Fuming, belt in hand, in fury at their door
Watching them in laughter rolling on the floor.

9

And then again, Sunday school, in smart new suits
That itched and set your neck on fire
Made it unlikely you'd ever sit still
Or keep the fidget out of your boots.
Him, being bigger, knuckling your arm,
Don't tell our mother, if we go there –
You dare – knuckling harder through gritted teeth –
Tell – our – mother – then that nervous laugh.
Released, you rushed to the lake's edge knowing
The ice was still thick and might yet bear weight.
Pushed forward – *You first* – his careful stutter.
Your feet clattered then you spun like a plate
Flat on your back careering and spinning
With him, smirking from the bank, *I'll tell our mother.*

Our mother's got a baby in her bed,
You hissed in the red funnel of his ear.
Don't talk daft how would it have got there –
Our dad would never let her, he said.
But so it was, leaving you in the middle
Between the first-born and our *baby boy:*
Never to be anything special
Ever again – the apple of no one's eye.
Always seeking a mother's approval
You knew you could never be too careful
Nor really disagree with anyone –
Cautiously stating a variable view,
You learnt to give it back with one hand
Having taken it – cap in hand – with the other.

11

Glass cabinets full of cups and saucers,
From which no tea will ever be drunk,
Trapping some still reverential air
For heirlooms, bibles and air-force trunks.
Antimacassars on the backs of chairs
Into whose lacey lines no heads will sink
And from whose seats none will ever stir
To poke the fire since the fire's not in.
Never to be used, this room's a shrine
Where photographs are dusted and set
For attention just once in a while:
Three boys' arms looped around each other's necks,
Mother in the middle with an awkward smile
With Father's shadow creeping up their legs.

12

We sifted through your drawers when you'd died,
Turning up postcards, bundles of letters,
Unopened tins of dominoes – hoping
We'd find nothing you'd not want us to see.
Your uniformed face in a seated crowd
In Ceylon, as it was, in *forty-three*
And Dorothy – in uniform too – looking
Assured and calm and so much better.
Then, among the paperclips and drawing pins,
That slim diary that your father wrote
In the thirties when you were just ten –
A short line each day as a brief note
To the future: *One of our better days*
Gifted a rabbit and a bunch of carrots.

13

January – the month that looks both ways –
But for you three just backward into the grave:
Father, son and mother *Together*
At last if we can believe that parcelling
These ashes and bones into one neat envelope
Amounts to a reunion:
A seasonal deathday gathering –
Welcome home – so much to catch up on.
And so much time, though there's no time there,
To put another log on the fire
Tell the dog to lie down and shush up,
Smile and say: So what have you been up to?
As if you'd just been away for a while
And we still had all the time in the world.

14

If you turn your forenames about,
You have – by chance – the same name as your
Great-grandfather who, we discovered,
Standing in the clag of a winter graveyard,
Died on the day that your brother was born
Albeit thirty years or so before.
Your brother's face went ashen when he saw
Some semblance of his future in the past.
We all look for signs of reassurance –
As he did then – but all that we can do
For each other is smile – or grimace –
Shrug our shoulders, rearrange the coping
And make sure the dead flowers have been replaced:
Hoping things don't turn about again too soon.

WARMING PAN

The copper's growing tarnished and the pad
That cushions it against the wall is green
Through taking on the tincture of the pan.

Walnut handle grained and rimmed at the neck,
A leather thong curls loosely at the head
On which a simple button sits erect.

And there it hangs, behind the door, and waits –
An heirloom to be passed on – of no use
But still an ornament to justify what's past.

It's fifty years, at least, since the hinge was lifted
And coals were heaped into the sooty case
Until the copper burned – too hot then to be touched –

And was carried – a simple vestal offering –
To the bed and passed across the sheets
In looping circles meant to warm not scorch

When all about the room was filled with frost:
Linoleum, brass bedstead and the pot
Cold rimed beneath the bed and still half full.

But that's all passed, and breath no longer sits
In plumes about the mouth, no patterns form
In icy fronds on windows anymore:

The warming pan's redundant and passed by
Until – dusted and polished now and then –
It's taken down and hung somewhere else instead.

ASH

The paper's ripped the surface of his under lip again;
His tongue explores the damage and the taste of blood
As he crushes the heat between his finger and his thumb
And drops it, between his legs, into the water.

It hisses once and dies as he scags a sheet of paper –
Last week's news – from the distempered nail
That's stuck into the wall and wipes himself.

It's over now and all that's left's a cloud
That dissipates as acrid and as seer
As all he's left behind for us to know:

Curt and undisclosed, he showed us nothing
And we gave nothing back for him to take
From us apart from silence and assumed respect.

We sat and listened – long afternoons that
Taught compliance and the slow unravelment of time
While we waited for something to happen.

But that was sixty years ago or more;
I no longer hear his voice and soon his face
Will disappear with me into that photograph

Of a man who smiled once, one sunny afternoon;
His wife relieved, his sons attendant risking
      smiles themselves
While someone let the shutter rise and fall.

He's buttoned up and ready to walk back
Down the yard, past the rhubarb and the plums,
To taste the sting of ash upon his throat awhile.

THURIBLE

A crepuscular ritual each time
He left the plot; unbuttoning his fly

And blessing the budding rhubarb roots
With one solid stream of piss, avoiding

The fronds of leaves – the better not to scorch
Them or betray his urinary ways –

But drilling down to the floppy, old man's
Rhizomes – like death itself – from which, in due course,

The pink flesh would arise ecstatically firm;
Forced under rusted buckets that let in the light

To tease their ruddy freshness as it – unfurling –
Pushed and strained, lifting gradually

The lid on a dark and distant underworld
Of phallic beasts and flouncing midnight tarts

Waiting to be tugged and wrenched and sliced
And boiled until the air was thick with the stew and tang

That – sugared – they would take with custard;
Arising from the clag, allotted and twice blessed.

TABLE

Upon which we place: photographs,
The cyclamen that's now in bloom again,
Boxes, an empty candlestick;
Those sundry bits that bob up and have
No place to go but can't be cast aside

Like the table itself: passed down
To me, my uncle's father's parents' gift
That no-one yet has sat around to eat
Or drink or pass the time of day;
It sits, has sat and ever will persist

Its drop-leaf shoulders hanging limp
Squatting like a toad – when I have passed it on –
In someone else's window, loft or shed;
Unused, unusable still filling space;
We can't allow the past to simply pass.

Impassively it sits and glares
Bleached by the sun and water stained
It's strangely un-neglected now by me;
No longer sitting in a room that's *kept for best*
It's becoming – like all things do in time –

Distressed, misused – no longer deified –
It's becoming now the thing itself:
A worthless piece of wood that's valued
More for the hands that never touched it
Than the job it's never done; sanctified

For being old, an emblem of the past
Devoid of purpose or of plot –
Apart that is of having been the thing
That they – our cautious forebears –might afford
To show that they'd made something of their lives:

A rustic table – hand-made – mahogany
Laid with a lace, embroidered cloth
On which they'd place photographs, candlesticks
And – in winter – a tender cyclamen
Just hopeful that the spring would come again.

CAP

And since it fits, I'll wear it – your old cap
That I captured as a token when you died
And dropped in a cupboard where I left

It, until this wet morning and me in need
Of something for the head and with nothing
Readily to hand, I saw it and thought

Why not? although these last few years I've thought
Why would I? not wanting to rim my head
And have it gripped tight and greased by you,

To feel the warm contortions of your brain
That harbour thoughts passed down in folds of cloth,
Part dented at the peak with your thumbprint.

But after all it only is a cap
And after one long morning in the rain
I find it fits me – slightly rakish when

I wear it tilted, and not four square like you –
Drenched and shrunk the tighter still, it's snug
And I've grown to feel it's mine, not yours.

Although I feel the impress of what was you,
I know that it's not you that I can smell
Mired in grease or stained still with pomade

The lining and the hat band and that
Little twist of feather where the seam
Is gathered in and stitched and held together

As I am now doffing my cap to you,
Paying heed but passing on, as commonplace
To me, Cliff, as once it was to you.

LUNDY, FASTNET, IRISH SEA

The sea is at my feet again – pewter
Grey and swooshing in the rocks,
Soughing through the pebbles, drawing back and
Dragging sounds out of my ears until I'm lost.

Cold drifting up my calves, clenching me
In stockings of mist – wet to the touch
If I dare to place a hand and have it clamped
In the grasp of coming ice.

There might have been a crash against the quay
Last night that caught me half awake and half
Asleep – sucked into the chasm of a
Waking dream that rocked me back again.

I cannot tune the radio or catch
My breath or touch the fading embers of
The day before I'm cast adrift and all
At sea upon this cabin tossed above the tide

Tucked athwart these steepling cliffs,
Holding my breath before the plunge of water
Tumbles me beneath the waves and draws me
Down into the murky darkness of no space

From which there are no words beyond the sound
That's drugging me asleep this one dull day
Of sparrows crouching in the eaves of masts
And light refracting zinc into a flat dark night.

HOSTAS

Achilles would have known the thrust
Of these tight leaves and felt the bite of gravelled shaft

As each sharp tip is forced up to the barb –
Adamantine – unable to retract

Unwilling to give ground, the leaves unfurl
Arriving with a shock when least expected

Like tarnished blood – the fingered coinage
Of deceit – the price that must be paid

For laying waste the sodden gateway
The dripping fount of rusted ancestry;

Shielded and helmeted yet unaware
Of ambush nor of if or when it comes

Enjoying now their moment in the sun;
The plume unfurls and riffles in the breeze

There is no present danger yet
No threat of being shredded, carved and dumped;

A tattered corpse wrapped in a threadbare flag
That's left to desiccate and rot all winter long

Until the legend can be told again
Of heroes – young in blood and of the earth –

Standing shoulders squared and rimed with frost
Eager and prepared though born to die.

DEMOBBED

Rain falls – for a day and halfway through the night –
His coat heavy and smelling still of war
But still he chose to walk – better that
Than the long wait at stations – making connections,
Hanging on to luggage racks and smoke –
He'd had enough of smoke – cordite and tobacco.

The air sweet after rain and after dawn
Across fields he barely knew – ankle deep in grass
That would be hay – scythed and dried and stacked –
The work that he knew best or would do
With hounds circling in the yard and nipping
At his hands for hard tack or aniseed.

Forty miles or maybe more – homing in
Without maps directed more by the scent
Of what he knew and where they were
Or had been – letters home and no response –
Expecting recognition and a smile
With so much that they'd tell him if they could.

Voices across the field trailing to where he stood
Leaning on a fence post choked with tears
That wouldn't come – better resting here than
Walking through the door unannounced and wet –
Watching them – unsuspecting – starting their day
Half aware of him – some stranger at the gate.

Feet rushing on ahead but his head still
Just taking stock – knowing it will never
Get better than this anticipation –
That welcomed back will never smell as clean
As this – savoured after all that's been and is to come –
Returned and not forgotten quite just yet.

Door pushed open dragging on the flags
Bag stowed up against the wall, he catches
His father's eye in the mirror – shaving –
Blade stropped, lather on his cheeks and water
Hot in that chipped enamel bowl – blue rimmed –
You're back then – blade in water – crunch of bristles

Taken from the cleft beneath the nose
Does your mother know? –finger poked in ear,
Rough towelling of the nape – water down the drain –
Did you walk? –nodding – voiceless not to break
The silence of return – You'll be wanting tea –
And more than that in losing all that's past.

CUFF LINKS

We're trying on his coats and jackets,
As if we've had a visitation from
A traveller in gentlemen's apparel
Just passing with a trunk of mohair, wool
And silken goods all guaranteed to please –
Just feel the weight of cloth – sheer quality.

Barely worn, no frays along the cuffs,
No stains upon the ties that hang fresh pressed
And certainly no grease marks at the neck.
He always kept himself so clean – loved clothes.

Such a pity then he never had a chance
To wear them in or out – just left them hanging
In protective bags, on hooks in cupboards
While he was otherwise engaged – with dying.

The leftover furnishings of a life
That's gone with just the faintest whiff of him
In the folds of cloth in which he once was wrapped.
He'd be so pleased to know you're having them –
A winter coat and jackets that fit me
As if our bodies were made for each other –
He'd hate to think of anything gone to waste.

Wary at first – usurping what was his
Or casting him aside, encased in cloth
That had the press of flesh now dead – unsure
That this is apt or that they suit or fit
Until I'm told That fits you perfectly –
Look in the mirror, which I don't but know
My living body animates them now
These dead things, left otherwise to hang
Until the moths have nibbled them with holes
And they're just fit for bin bags and the tip.

And in this way, we justify ourselves,
Pretend that it's not happening to us;
It's someone else's life that's over, consigned
To the past while our future, like these cufflinks,
Their little intimacies still intact,
We place upon the mantle-shelf until another day.

CONTEXTUAL

My hand upon your head grew still
From stroking you to sleep
As your breath grew steadier and deep;

Half an hour or more on my knees
Your willing supplicant eager
To get back on my feet and do some jobs

Though what they were and what their worth
I could no more tell either then or now.
My hand lifted and hovered, cupped

Along the contour of your fragile skull –
Warm with the heat of your seething brain
And smelling of that sweet shampoo and scalp.

I levered myself upright and stepped back –
Keen to make no noise and slip away
Leaving you to the safety of the night.

I turned to go and made one silent step:
Stroke my hair – your voice insistent barked,
My breath was stifled, hoping you'd fall back.

I mean it – stroke my hair – I'm not asleep yet.
Like a voice that's coming from beyond the years
To make me turn my head and turn to stone

You texted me last night – thirty years later –
To say you're full of cold and couldn't talk.
I texted back and hoped that you'd sleep well.

INTIMACIES

Late August – three or more decades ago –
With you and me and she who loved you
Sitting drinking in the slanting sun

You at your colouring book while we talked –
Effaced from memory – some catching up
About the month now past and the return

From travels to our work routines again
About which you were oblivious
As we were of her need to kill herself

In due time – though niggling then within her skull
As was yours to empty soon your bladder
I would concur but not before we'd done

With whatever we'd got left to say
Until your desperation – not hers – showed
And I lifted you off the bench over

To that flower bed – late afternoon
With no one there to see as I held you –
Pants around your ankles cradled above

Roses and petunias – still talking
Over my shoulder as you giggled at
The boldness of it all – *No one will see*

I said – *Just go* – as surely then you did
Before that reassuring *poo* prepared
Me for what followed next to help the roses grow.

VANISHING POINT

There are no rules of perspective
Just a random collision of shapes,
The occasional confluence of forms.

Telegraph wires sag between posts
And dip aslant the field's edge:
Four lines make space then coalesce.

A puff of smoke makes haste to dissipate
Moving against the telegraph lines
Away from the sun that spreads golden

As the dawn gives way to morning
And the sun itself arrives to darken
The outline of trees against the winter sky.

There are thin lines of clouds
Once dark now scratching light across the blue
That begin to slip higher and slide away.

From above, this field would hold its lines too
Where the winter wheat shows green
In rows that bank and gather in hollows.

A pheasant stands on one foot, head cocked,
Having scurried to a halt
Cautious, it moves – just one step at a time –

Along the fence line, blithely unaware
Of the watcher who frames him
Through a window that is strangely set askew.

COMPLICIT

Year's end or year's start,
We find two shrunken heads on the lawn –
Eyeless and earless – conspiring in
Their silence to leave us with the guilt.

The best we can do is keep it to ourselves,
Clear them away and carry on as before.

The tree has been taken and the jackdaws have returned,
All hunched shoulders and blank faced acknowledging
Their part in all this but keeping their distance;

We watch them pecking at the eyes
Of one that's just arrived here overnight.

If this goes on, we'll have a cache
Too many to dispose of when they come.
The pile is growing higher every day.

And now the children are involved,
Smiling every time we look surprised
Or pushing sticks into the plushy flesh.

We've asked them to desist
But they just shrug and smirk at one another
Then meekly walk away.

DRAGONFLIES

All eyes, they're coming closer as we sit
And watch them watching us
Plated and jointed and armour bright
In the late morning sun.

If they needed a name we'd give them one
But they are beyond that –
In the kingdom of the flat lake and swamp
The four-winged beasts do not.

We can hear them as they wheel towards us –
Rudder sharp and banking
On veined wings that whirr as the sun catches
And flashes and makes us blink.

Farther out, above the bronze bright surface
Patina of the lake
The damselflies are weaving a thick gauze
And making the air shake.

There are fish too – indolent in the shade –
Rising with mouths agape
Then falling back into the circles that they've made –
We watch them dissipate.

And this will be the morning of your life
Before you give them names:
Broad bodied chasers and Southern hawkers
Will never be the same

As these monsters with their goggle eyes
That craned around corners
To inspect, dissect, reject and surprise
Before your grown-up years.

MUSÉE D'ORSAY

You'll not remember this, utterly bored
By Gauguin and eager for a bun,
You're sitting on the floor, knees in the air
And glowering at our backs: *I can't take much
          more of this.*

Ever the educator, I make you look
Into the Breton cottage window and
Imagine what's inside on that wet day;
You're not that much impressed until I show

A tiny speck of red dabbed on the glass
And – desperate for some respite from your gloom –
Suggest you hold your finger up – *don't touch* –
To blot it out and see what happens then.

Though *pretty dull* already, it grows yet duller still
And illuminates your next few minutes there;
Independent now your finger held aloft
With one eye tight shut, you're turning out the lights

In rural France but find Tahiti hard –
Those slabs of colour and those women's breasts
Need no obliteration from your thumb –
So you're off and searching galleries on your own.

Your mother turns and grows distraught – you're lost
To art and for three minutes we fear the worst,
Panic and range like Breton chickens
Frantically hoping you've not been led astray.

Which, of course, you've not. Recovered, you've won:
Since we are so relieved, you've earned your bun
And we've seen quite enough pictures for one day
As you lead us – smiling – to the next café.

BRYLCREEM

The white stuff plastered on my head, and I was blessed:
Those springy hairs laid flat
Gave me the air – at seven and a half –
Of an accountant at his rigid ease.

You were, of course, distressed – beside yourself –
Placated by a plastic duck that quacked
Ventriloquised by your mother,
The better to distract you with its beady eyes.

You'd rather not be there – no more would I –
Preened up to play the part we just *sat still*
And waited for the bearded man to guillotine
His film, wring the neck of his brassy lens
And, disappearing within his big, black cape,
Make the world go flash and flare, and you to cry again.

BEYOND KITSCH

Because our local vicar tickled palms
And had an easy Welshman's lilt and leer,
We walked two miles to Sunday morning church
And two miles back relieved but still bemused
By what our little ritual walk might mean.

What was it that they wanted us to be –
A middle-class simulacrum of themselves
Subservient to the specious word of God,
Or was it just some time that they'd won back
While we played out their simple pious part?

But now, I guess, we know there is no God
So all those Sunday mornings made no sense
Beyond their wish to do the best they could
As parents seeking to insure against
The loss of some control in changing times.

Yet maybe still – within our pagan age –
There is some routine purpose to be served
By mouthing out those platitudes again
And shoring up the present with the past
Remembrance of some words that make no sense.

When Elvis sings *You were always on my mind* –
Not in a service station or lift shaft –
But as the curtains close before the flames
The words have gone from nonsense back to sense
And make the simulacrum whole again.

SWING

Higher than I might have wished but never out of sight,
I glimpsed a world beyond – over the garden fence –
Where tinkers called to sharpen knives
And bread men bearing baskets
Came with crusts that – buttered – made my jaws ache
With the sheer delight and slaver of it all.

Rocking gently at first, the metal hoop squeaked
And gulped as the pressure on the seat pushed me
        further back
Then – flexing at the knee and pulling back my feet –
The rock became a sway became a surge
And now I'm up and flying, clinging to the chains
That stain my hands and print them with a tang

That hangs about the hollows of my throat.
Paint flaking – bubbling and blistering from the posts –
Much taller than they ever should have been:
A derrick poking up above the shed – set in concrete
And never likely to tip or skew or throw me
To the ground – though bruising knees was

Always likely when – going just too far –
I'd need to stop, jump clear and right myself,
Allow the whoosh to settle in my ears
And swallow hard to hold back all that slew;
The aftertaste of lunches and cream teas
Advancing fast in green before my eyes.

I'd had enough, the swing became a curse:
The chain looped up and tied about the post,
The grass grew back where once my feet had scuffed.
The seat began to splinter then and rot.
It had to go. Recycled into posts and props and scrap
Till no one knew what once was any more.

SEPTEMBER 6TH

This is where it started: with one long scream;
Breathless and insistent and alarmed
By all this otherness of eiderdowns
And blankets, rubber sheets and steaming cloths,
And that enamel bucket with a lid that clanged
To keep what's wasted always at arm's length.

You're sleeping now, I guess, and I'm allowed
To watch you tucked against *my* mother's breast
Her head inclined but asking me to join
Her in the triumph and to share her love
With you, sister, a word I must have tried
For the first time that day – and found it strange.

They'd ask me – grandparents, uncles and aunts –
What I thought of you – your brand-new sister –
As if I'd have some well-turned epigram,
Some *bon mot* neatly honed to offer them:
She reminds me, creased by birth and reddened,
More of a pickled beetroot than a girl.

So precocious and yet so silent and abashed
By all this access to a hidden world
Of blood, obstetrics and something underhand
To which they all had entry while I did not;
Discomforted by their smirks and the grapes
And the bottles of yellow fizz in cellophane.

Eventually, they left us to get on with it:
Growing up, leaving and now, coming back
To where we were; the room is as it was;
The accoutrements and personnel have changed
But what she offered me of hers that I might share,
Remains which I with gratitude give back to you.

CHARLIE'S DEAD

The fringe of scalloped lace no longer hangs
Beneath the pleated hem of knee-length skirt
And if it did, who'd think to nudge and wink
Or decorously hint that honour might be lost
Unless she were to hitch up from the waist
That trailing edge – and claim her modesty again.

I guess it was the only whiff we had of sex:
A world of clasps and straps and stocking tops
That gave us access to the prize itself –
Of what that was we'd only get a glimpse
When older cousins called or if the girl next door
Bent down to tie her shoe or shift her breast.

Later, queueing for *Biology* or *Maths*
We'd show our ignorance to those who said they knew;
Attended coffee bars and spoke with girls themselves,
Had cigarettes and condoms in their bags
And passed around those pictures from *Parade*
At which we smirked and held our breath – then blushed.

Fumbled embarrassment, the shame and fear
Of being, finally, found out by those
Who label lack of confidence *Queer*
At which we'd bridle, blush a deeper shade of red
And learn to lurk in darkened corners settling –
Once we'd plucked our courage up – for the girls
      they'd left behind.

So, Dad, we never did get round to that
Little chat about the birds and bees.
You'd threaten – now and then – to fill me in;
I could see it coming when you closed the door
And churned loose change in pockets as you
      stared perplexed
Then cleared your throat – before deferring it again.

I was, of course, relieved each time you walked away
And – more so – when you said, before I left for good,
We had our little chat – you know not what to do
Which eventually, of course, I did – through trial and
      abject error –
And so I left my sons to work out for themselves
What – now that *Charlie's dead* is dead – they'll
      make of it.

Fumbled embarrassment, the shame and fear
Of being, in the end, found out by those
Who'd call their lack of confidence the same as mine
At which they'd bridle, blush a deeper shade of red
And learn, I hope – their time come round at last –
To simply walk away and shrugging try again.

ACCADEMIA

We learn to find new intimacies
Beneath the belly's folds and fronds.

The sculptor's hand quarters the stone,
To conjure up a moment out of time,
And finds what always had been there:
A careless arm thrown gracefully
Across a naked breast.

And now, in the heft of all too solid flesh
We fumble to recall our former shapes:
To chisel out with tenderness
These latter forms of love.

A jawline puffed with age remains
As straight and clean as once it was
While teeth stained yellow yet may shape a smile.

The sculptor – with a lover's coaxing – strokes,
His fingers combing clean the marble dust,
Allows the hump of Venus to arise
Or weighs the loaded ball sac in his palm.

So we with fingers intertwined at night
In darkness rediscover shapes
In cusps of buttock, clefts of breast
Where once we knew our other selves to be.

And even in the midnight breath that claws
At air with rasping gasps and snores
We hear, beneath it all, the soft blown breeze
Of what was once and always will be – love.

BYRE

You said *It's a good bed not too soft*
And we are learning – this week – to sleep hard
Snug under rafters and tucked tight beneath
The scratch of mice or the tug of wind.
Afloat in space for once and on the edge
Of a valley suspended in clean air
Quite unaware of the drop beneath
Our feet or where they'll lead us when we wake.

We are uncoupling our very selves
And shuffling back to from where we came
Before we were lost in that confusion
Of crossings and turnings and never standing still.
It's taken days this learning to sleep hard
Beyond ourselves and back unto each other.

HANDLE

Well before the wheel, someone – passing food
Or drink from an open hearth and fearful
That the touch would scald the calloused fingers
Or be just too hot to hold and blister
On the way from hand to lip – invented
This little twist of clay, this loop of dried mud
To help us keep our distance from the hurt.

So, this morning, a timeless ritual that
We've observed – honouring our past, and theirs –
You passed to me the cup and said *Take care,
It's hot, I'll put it down and then you can –*
As I did – *pick it up* – safely unhurt
Holding the fragile stem complacently
Between my thumb and two firm fingers.

These little acts of love will be all that will remain
When we have left the hurt behind and settled,
Beside the fire, at evening or at dawn,
Counting another day to come or gone
And sharing what remains – and all we had –
After the trappings and the circumstance,
A simple handle passed with care from you to me.

PURLEY ROAD

Blemished, we bought it cheap, a crocus pot
With a perfect lid and a handle twist of clay
That sat mid-shelf holding itself quite still
Until – lifted – the light lid fell and smashed.

So many pieces shattered on the hearth
– Some no more than dust –
Needing to be regathered and reformed,
Balanced and made into that easeful shape again.

I'm searching on my knees to make sense of it:
Scrabbling around until I've found all the bits
Bar one – the painted line that rims the lid
And makes the circle whole – is lost

Until I recognise how wide the fallout's been,
How distant from the break each piece has flown,
How far my eye must travel to recover
Everything and find the missing piece.

And when I do, it's gravity that lets me down:
Balancing the parts with fingers gummed with glue,
I make a collage of the lid – folded
Fragments hanging on that make a ragged dome

Which, in the end, looks like some mutant beast
Of dribbled glue that's made the two into
Just one pot, it's lid – crookedly askew – stuck fast
Never to be parted and welded to the shelf.

OAK SWILL

Cleft lengthwise, we are peeling apart
Riven into strips, we're splintering
As brittle as eggshells and ready to snap.

We walk, knitting a path around ourselves
That binds us in a knot that will not slack
No matter how hard we pick – until at last

It's all been said and the parts that make us one –
Fine taws and thick spelks held in a firm bool –
May yet fasten into something whole again.

Softened by the touch of hands and lips,
We start to weave the fabric of the swill
Into a bowl to hold what we had thought was lost.

We're making it – imperfectly – from wood
That's old yet still unseasoned and likely
To split and crack unless we both take care –

Knowing that even after all this time,
We're still about the learning of the craft;
Making what we can and hoping it will last.

SCAFFOLDING

Encased in bars, the light's subdued;
There is a hush about the house now they have gone
And we've learnt to pad around like monks
Under the bell of the ringing rods:

We're piecing together their language now:
Vertical standards shanked into a base plate,
Wedded to each other by ledgers – transoms
Bearing boards, cross-braced diagonals, guard rails

Dependent on the couplers to clinch them tight,
We watched as they appeared in hand – tossed high
And landing on an upturned palm – clasped,
Bolted tight, checked – singles, right-anglers, swivels.

The case was soon complete, and they had gone
Leaving us enmeshed in angles – cloistered
In stillness where once there was but air –
Temporarily arrested – held in place.

FABRICATION

Betrayed by the cockerel that's acting dead,
He sweeps the missing feathers from the path
And looks upon the wreckage that he's made;

For him, the bird is dead and Christmas too
Along with any hope that he'll be spared
The strap and early banishment to bed.

But after all, he thinks, *the bird deserved it* –
Baring claws and pecking at his doves –
He had to take a swipe and scare it off.

The stolid lump's inert upon the path
As he rehearses lines that will placate
His mother and save him from his father's ire.

He's learning now the art of subterfuge,
Of how to crimp and curl a tale until
There's little chance that he will take the blame.

Of course, the bird was dead when he arrived
As he – all innocence – was passing by
And there it was – distressing but no fault

Of his – there'd be no evidence, no marks
Left smeared upon the broom and no feathers
Stirring in the breeze – he'd get away with it.

These lessons learnt in childhood will cohere
And teach the way to manufacture lies
That when embroidered make a tapestry

To wrap around him when he's old and frail:
The way things were is as they might have been
As he sits and fabricates another tale

What can I tell you now? There's nothing left to say
And after all, the bird revived itself
So when his mother came to check the facts

It was on its feet and pecking grains again,
Scratching in the dust in search of meal
And crowing unalarmed by death itself.

BEBOP

It's 1947 and I'm waiting
For my cue – to come out of the shadows
And play my solo alongside them all.

Although they're trying very hard
I'm not ready yet to step up to the mark
And shuffle my handful of scrappled notes

That they – in time – will bundle into shape
Leaving me to improvise around the tune
They've gathered into random sheaves and lines

That make no ready sense to me at all
As I stand in the half light of the wings
Squinting at all those dots and flicking tails.

Meanwhile, he's letting fly in one great torrent
And cascade of pent-up grunts and gasps
That leaves him breathless and unspent again

While she, hoping that something will stick this time
To keep her from this ritual *sturm und drang,*
Hears the tail beat and the bebop line

Of Charlie Parker playing *My old flame*
Beneath the hum and pulse of radio valves
That in the end will lull her fast asleep.

So, every time I hear them play again –
With Miles, impatient waiting for his break –
I'm eased myself into that other place
Of promise, love and – inevitably – shame.

CROSS-BRED

They've made me what I am and now they praise
My docility – my willing compliance –
As if I had a choice in the matter.

In truth, I'm hiding from myself –
Dragging this plaited tail and matted coat
Under tables – sliding under benches –

Pressing my eye against this skirting board
To admire its grain of wood, that well-turned leg,
Abutted timbers – chamfered – held in place.

I'm learning to avoid the betrayal
Of puddles – the insincerity of glass –
The cold appraisal of another day

I'm sleeping less – though often I'll contrive
To close my eyes and act as if I am
Until they poke me in the ear or jab

They've made me – so I'll not retaliate
I have a reputation to maintain:
There is some reassurance in pebbles

The sweet oblivion of wind and rain
And noises off: the crash of waves, their voices
That make no sense apart – that is – for words

I've come to recognise – occasional
But welcome – instructional, I guess,
I act as if I know just what they mean, which they

Appreciate – delighted – they congratulate
Themselves and tell me I am a *good boy*
Though what that means I'm yet to understand.

GUILTY PLEASURES

Overloaded and heavy with the fullness
Of promise, I could not resist stopping
To open the sack and admire their cloudy swellings
Impassively heaving at my eager eyes.

Given a gentle – then more vigorous – rub,
They would bloom purple or chafe russet gold
Yielding to the press of finger and thumb
If I cupped one tightly in my palm.

Then, lifting its softness to my lips,
I'd bite along the dorsal crease and
Halve it from crown to muddy stem,
Working the flesh with a probing tongue

Until the sharp pit struck back and drew blood
That, mingling with the sweet juices, pulsed out
One great drool of sticky, silky pulp
In oozes leaking from the corner of my mouth.

Clamped tight between teeth: a ruddy lipstick
Poked out from full and flaring fronds,
The ribbed and rigid stone triumphant still,
Spat over hedge tops, tumescent in the grass.

BRIDLEPATH

This was our route into the underworld,
Although we never knew it at the time
As we looked for minnows in the stream
And tracked through rat runs of hawthorn,
Underwear and discarded magazines,
Lugging a sodden sack of dead fox back
Up the track where the neck would be cut open
And the contents spilt wet upon the lawn.

The milk never tasted the same, we said,
Although the tarnish was more of graphite
And the press of pencils on shiny sheets
Of clean lined paper into which the ink,
One day, would not – determinedly – run.

Stopping on the way today and looking back –
Fifty years – down the path, I saw all clear
And sanitised snaking down the leeside
Of a wall along which women walk dogs
And nod in recognition as I pass –
Not of myself so much as of some
Other self – an ageing man who should know
Better than to stop to piss where children
And the unconsolable might walk.

OFF THE RAILS

Climbing the embankment – heavy with April dew –
He tucks his bag deep in the blackthorn bush,
Straightens his tie and presses on upwards
Into the morning light of this last day.

And you are on your way to meet him now,
Strangely unaware – just then – of how you would
Remember the cast of his eye and the hunch
Of his shoulders gathered tight against the line.

Making himself ready, he removes his coat,
Folds it over – once or twice – and makes a pillow
That he's placing now across the rail
Onto the sleeper where his head will fit.

You're halfway through your shift and time is sweet
With foxes in the briars and rabbits
Scuttling down the slopes over which you ride
As signals press you onwards – *right away* – today.

Immaculate in everything he's done,
He lies down snug into the hollow
That he's made to nest him in the ballast
And hold him for the moment when his head rolls free.

Sun glints off the rails to catch you unawares
And make you squint into the morning haze
Where – coming off the bend – you see him there,
At first a hump of sack and then a head.

He looks up and knows that soon it will be gone:
This long, dull ache sends creases through his brain
And will not depart – no matter what they say –
However much is promised as relief.

You can see him now and the clear affront
Of his eyes staring back and up at you.
Your hand goes to the brake – but stops short –
As you hurtle ever onwards with the breath thick
       in your chest.

The head's gone but the body's still intact:
His two arms tucked tight between his legs,
His knees curled upwards gathered to his chest
With the rumble and the rattle fading in the rails.

And for him it's all over – stuck in a trance
You see nothing but his eyes and the smack
Of the wheel across his slender neck
As the rails unfurl in fields of parcelled green.

*

She rises from her nest alarmed as you shriek
Around another bend – primed, duct heavy
To lay – later – a clutch of buff specked eggs
This warm spring day with blossom on the breeze.

The pulsing numbness – leaving *you* for dead –
Is broken by another slap and smack
That leaves her smeared and yolk bright on the glass
Of your approaching locked-in cabin cell.

LOOK AFTER ONE ANOTHER

Was your talismanic envoi as we closed
Down each phone call – in my case, a duty done
But in yours a ritual repetition
Of all you'd asked the week before.

Was it to secure a fond recollection:
And do you know – I'll always remember –
The last thing he said was …
Or was it to ensure you'd be there again

Next time – *Could be better* – but still relieved
To be present with those questions well-rehearsed
Of how the children fared and where I'd been
Until, accordingly, we'd done our bit?

Just lately, since your world's shrunk back again,
I've noticed that you've stopped saying it
And whereas the ending of our calls
Would start minutes before we reached the point

When we'd stop – *Bye then, bye, look after one …*
Never trailing off – now they simply end
As if you've had enough of this clinging on
To a body that does nothing for you

But – in revolt – does what it will and when
Regardless of your needs or circumstance
And takes some looking after. So what's the point
Of making sure the record's straight, the i's

Are dotted and the tea – grown cold upon your lap –
Is drunk before the next one comes along.
Looking after – and before – to be at one
With each and other but mostly just yourself.

ANDROMEDA

You'll know me by the chains about my wrist
That bound me to him out of loyalty
Or some infection in the blood
That he was well aware would keep me here
Attendant to his moods and every whim.

I served him well – but never satisfied –
His appetite was greater than his needs
And I the willing supplicant
Forever on my knees or at his back
Removing thorns and washing clean his wounds.

He's sleeping now but way beyond my grasp
For I've been turned to face the other way
And only catch the movement of his breath
In the rise and fall of the tattered shawl
They've placed about his shoulders and his neck.

This is my time – and time enough to kill
Then make my exit swiftly and secure –
If only I had kept the talons sharp
Or even clung on to the combs I use
To tease the knots from what remains of hair.

There will be others that follow after me
To keep a vigil, rectify the runes
And pay dull homage to a truth that's past
Which only stays by dint of ancient rules
That trust has long abandoned and ignored.

In the end, we're always on our own
Shackled to some rock of circumstance
That drives us to maintain our presence here
And keep a watchful eye on those we know
Will gladly take advantage if we don't.

BICYCLE

The past smells of creosote and rusty nails
In the shed where everything's been recycled:
Sideboards, cut down to make bedside cupboards,
Became the repository for brushes,
Whose bristles never stiffen, jars and cans.

The kitchen cabinet – sleek enamel
And quite the thing in 1956 –
Stacked high and wide with stuff that *might come in:*
Brylcreem jars, labelled, full of nails and screws,
A spring balance that's lost its will to spring
And folded, varnished rules that measure out in inches
The distance that we've come and where we've yet to go.

But the centrepiece, propped aslant the bench,
Your bicycle, draped in curtains, oiled and rustless,
Since that day you cycled home and left it
And turned to bowls, *pub lunches* and the rest –
While its chain grew slack, and its hub forgot to tick.

And now you're parked yourself, imagining
What's stacked in corners or still arranged in drawers
You'll never open – and how the bike fares
That you'll never see again but whose tyres,
This sultry afternoon of flies and cups of tea,
I'm pumping up at your request as if to prove
That nothing perishes or will be wasted in the end.

TREE

Pressed into service to delineate a spot
Whose spurious provenance has always been in doubt,

It wavers in the breeze – these hundred years
Are coming to a close; dismembered,

The outer branches flutter to the ground
Before the amputation of dead limbs

That fall like drumbeats deep into the earth,
Or – rolling over – come to rest at last.

It's over but the taking down takes time
Since presence has a hold on all that's been

And space vacated is an act of will –
Like life itself – as precious as a dream

That's lost on waking but whose faint impress
Is with us for the rest of each short day

Until we turn to find it's gone
Like that attendant beech we've always known

Would be there marking out our passage in
And swaying at our passing out again

Remarked upon more likely when it's gone
Than like a father when it's always there.

CREAM

You're dabbing benedictions on his head
– Pater noster, qui es in hospitali –

Small white blobs of analgesic cream
That you stroke into his scalp until it gleams.

Idly going nowhere, just waiting
For a visitation or a sleep,

Easing the irritation and the itch,
His thick and horny fingers are raking at his scalp.

Until it seems he's hurtled through a hawthorn hedge
That's scratched and scabbed his pate with tines and barbs

And forks and thorns grabbing and slashing and crowning
Him with this criss-cross path of random lines

Just waiting for you to soothe his wounds
– Fiat voluntas sua in terra –

And leave him – blessed – your hand upon him still
With a gentle parting pat upon the skull.

CHTHONIC

I hold your hand to help you cross the road
But you aren't ready to go there just yet
And grip me back as tightly as you can –
Wary of slipping into sleep again.

Marked by the purple kohl of seeping blood,
Your eyes peer at me before rolling back
Once more into the damask darkness
And the thud of your own impassive heart.

So soft that hand, uncalloused by labour
Now that there's nothing left to grasp and cleave
You merely cling – onto the blanket's hem,
The sheet's clean edge and – now – your daughter's hand

Gesturing – maybe – when I ask you if
You can hear me when I'm talking to you –
Fatuously – about a world to which
You might come back – though less intact this time.

Your breath is raking at your chest and claws
Great lumps of phlegm into the clotted air
While your blackened tongue fondles each sweet draught
Then draws it down into your flooded lungs.

You're taking your time – to inhabit dreams
That – you told me just two weeks ago – were
Plentiful and yet unremarkable
And not – in truth – to be remarked upon;

That secret underworld of memory
And lost desires – the fantasies that float
And bubble up only to subside or pop,
Dissolve and disappear at once on waking.

And this, I think, is what you'll not want – waking –
Preferring soon – your body blown to bits –
To sink back on the pillow and forget
As I loose your hand and watch you cross the road alone.

SHAKING HANDS

Is all we've ever done on parting:
You taught me the value of a firm handshake
To rectify the lassitude within.

To proffer not a hand that's limp and damp
But one that's complemented with an eye
That looks steadfastly at the one's we leave.

It is, of course, a sham – an artifice
That covers up the confidence we lack
And makes due recompense for what we're not.

We could have hugged each other once or twice
But never did – preferring to keep our distance
To wish each other well and trust we'd meet again.

Until today when, your hand cold upon the sheet,
I slipped my hand into your palm and pressed
And felt the limpness of a life that's gone

Before we'd had the chance to say those words
We'd never said of love and death and afterwards.
And now it's all too late, it's slipped away

As I did yesterday – saying I'd be back
To see you soon just like I always did
But knowing that you'd gone already

And when I returned there was no hand to shake,
No gestures left to fabricate a lie
And only this unmitigated truth:

We lived within each other's lives for years
And never knew more of what we were or felt
Than what a simple handshake could impart

Take care – look after one another –
Keep in touch – hello stranger – I've been worried
To death about you – and now you're gone.

GIVING DEATH

We labour to be born and labour to be dead.
No longer in the delivery room, we're posted back
Return to sender labelled, patched and stamped

With gore or maybe merely blessed
As he is now, battened under blankets
With a slight bruise, head upon the pillow,

The shallowness of breath fading
As we – watching – sense it's seeping clear away
Into that airy nothingness without.

Until he's back – yawning like a cat that
Suns itself, turns to face the light and drifts
Once more into untroubled sleep.

So it was, as the evening swelled and passed
We thought he would be gone before too long
But – hours later – he's there – labouring to be
        dead again.

His breath no longer rasping, his eyes are mostly shut
And we are caught halfway between the urge
To let him go and the need to hold him back.

Maybe there's something we need to do alone.
We let him be, half close the door and part
Wondering if by morning he will have given death.

PIETA

A little choreography of hands:
His daughter lifts his leaden head, props him
And drapes the tubes more loosely at his neck,
Rearranges the sheets and holds his hand:
Their right hands locked together, her left one
Rests upon his shoulder that she strokes.

His wife – on the other side of the bed –
Is stroking his left shoulder and his brow
While her left hand rests upon his leg
Moving it occasionally though he does not –
Apart from the movement up and down
Of his chest and the flicker of his breath.

I'm sitting at his bed's feet, my left hand
Holding the ridged bones and pads of his
While my other hand is resting – quite still –
Upon his wife's arm – we do not stir
Until my daughter texts to wish us well
And asks me then to squeeze her grandad's hand.

Eventually, we part and leave him to himself
Until, on our return he's gone; blood drained
From his face and that O-gape of surprise
That is only death catching him unawares
And leaving him there – unnaturally still
With us looking at him – and him so far away.

The women touch his shoulders, stroke his head
With plaints of reassurance and dry tears
While I, keeping my distance still, watch him
Half expecting him to turn again, blink
And wonder where he is. I touch his hand
Then say *Goodnight*, turn on my heels and leave.

IN FLAMES

Abhorring waste and mess, on Christmas Day
My father – having opened his presents –
Would gather the paper – screwed into balls –
Don his hat and scarf and incinerate it all.

Another Christmas going up in smoke
Before the turkey and the sausage rolls:
He'd saved the world from clutter and the air
Was sweet with burnt paper and soft ash.

Today, I did the same in memory of him:
Ten days dead and waiting to be gone
Impassively alone while we are at our feasts,
I took our wrappings to the compost heap

And set it all alight, watching those black feathers
Flap and turn upon the breeze and drift away
Over tree-tops into the wintry sky
As the flames crackled against the dark earth.

Eventually, they died down glowing still
Until I earthed them over, made a heap –
A little mound of soil where I had been
With a smell that lingered as I made my way indoors.

AFTERWARDS

You came to me in a dream last night –
Not you, of course, but what I'd made of you
Sleeping against the hush and suck of the sea.

It was you all right, not your old self –
The one I'd seen last of all – but the one
From long ago: middle-aged and cocksure

Telling us what to do and what was right;
No middle-ground just the push of self
That made me want to scream – boxed in by the

Sheer force of will that made you what I said,
Kindly, when you'd died: *a man of firm views*
With whom we agreed to differ and keep

Not *our counsel* but our distance – in fear
That you would turn and vent your vitriolic spleen
In splatches on those who disagreed.

So hard, to ease this passage out of life
Without giving ground to sanctimonious
Respect: it's what's expected not the truth

Since you're not here to argue now your case –
As if in death you'd gained some reason and
Some way of seeing someone else's point

Of view, the capacity to say:
I see what you mean, you must forgive me
For what I said and thought, I'm a changed man

And no longer what you ever thought I was.
How neat to have it all resolved, instead
Of which I'm left – the sea still at my back –

Remembering the dream and what you were:
Self-centred, self-absorbed and – sometimes – cruel:
So sorry, now, I can't dream otherwise.

CLOCK

Of which we pay no heed, above the door
Long stopped but worthy of that occasional
Riposte – It keeps the very best of time:
Accurate twice each day at two past three.

Arrested – in limbo – between what might
Have been and what is yet to come *Always*
Too late or too early for any thing
Yet faithfully attendant on the hour.

Time stops eventually – as it has for you –
Unremarkable as our kitchen clock:
Still present but serving no purpose
Apart from those of us for whom the tick

Is ever present and the tock a constant complement
From which we can't escape until we come
One day – like you – to notice that it's gone:
The hands no longer moving and the pulse

Quite dead upon the counterpane or quilt
And – at last – no day – or night – at all
But simply something that – at once – has stopped
Just like that clock – and you – devoid of sound

Or substance and the regularity of tick
That's followed in due season by the tock
Whilst those of us who do remain have time
Upon our hands with nothing left to come.

INTERMENT

And after all's been said, we touch your box
As if we're shaking hands or tapping on
Your shoulder as you turn to walk away

Hoping you might look back – instead of which
You've turned long since to dust and this flat box
Is no more you than the name that's stamped on top.

Uncompromising as the rain of this
Cold April day; eleven o'clock
As you would wish and as you hoped

You're planted – snug as a bean – alongside
Those who went before – we'll leave you soon behind
Although we vow that we'll return, place flowers,

Erect another stone for others to
Compute the years and rearrange the names
And shape a story no one then will know.

All's safe – the loyalty of sons, those words
We'd wished had been unsaid, the memory
Of love and war and anger and mistrust

All confined within a simple six-foot plot:
There are no reunions there, no glasses
Raised to fortify or warm or cheer.

We toss our handfuls of dry earth on top
To get you started, bed you in and cover
Up the plaque – your name and all those years.

There are tears and handshakes and promises.
Though when we passed you later – driving back –
We barely paused and knew that hole already had
        been filled.

FOURTH POCKET

It never comes immediately to hand –
That key or wallet, phone or credit card:

We're ready to leave, to pay or just call home
And reach unconsciously for it

Only to find it's not there or there or
Even – penultimately – there but here

At last – bulking large – tucked where we knew it was
Since – after all – we'd put it there ourselves

Conscious of the need but failing to call
It to mind from the silt of memory

The accumulated dross of a day
Through which we've passed completely unaware

Of what's been happening beneath the surface:
All those decisions made unwittingly

By something else instead – that other self
That's passed so closely by we've almost felt

Its stranger's breath brush gently on our cheek
In passages and doorways where we've tried

To push and pull and push and pull once more
To find – at last – it opens to reveal

What we had half suspected all along:
That someone's playing tricks to confound us here again.

BLANKET

By morning the checked blanket is still there
Creased and folded in the chair
Where I left it – fever filled – the night before.

If I were an artist, I would try to catch
The way it's held my slumpen shape
And kept it – engraven – overnight

But I don't have the lines so must try words
To fit the folds and flutes of fabric:
The way the tassels crimp and curl

And how the check becomes unchecked
And blues – no longer netted – hide behind
The whites while red threads scribble down the arms.

This is the shape of the feverish dream –
Cast aside as I stumbled to my bed but
Rising now – refreshed – I see it as it is:

A blanket to be folded then put away
Like sickness and the dread of ending
Thus – deferred again until another day.

HOMAGE

That morning I was late getting away
And knew I'd be missing my appointed slot
Unless I pressed myself and caught up time
Along the lanes – cutting through the backs of towns
Past football grounds, industrial estates,
Shuttered kebab vans and old men trimming lawns.

Accelerating, moving through the gears
And climbing upwards into open space,
I sensed I could win back the time I'd lost
Until, rounding a bend, I balked, changed down
And joined a line of cars moving slowly
Through heavy candles on the chestnut trees.

Burnished copper beeches, a clock face set
At noon fell now within the ambit
Of my gaze but – impatient – craning forward,
I looked to see where the road might straighten
To give me passing room to get beyond
The slow mid-morning progress of those less urgent
        than myself.

The one in front – a loaded minibus,
A charabanc for the recently retired
With – ahead of that – some low-slung sleek affair
That took its time to take in all that was
In fields and hedgerows on this one May day
Through which I now was passing at their pace.

At first it was the darkness of their suits
And then the steadfast angle of their heads
That made me see what first I'd missed
About their measured passage through the lanes
And the certain destination from which
One of their number never would return.

And May was everywhere as we slowed
To let the traffic hasten past our nose
Towards the motorway and distant depots,
Meeting rooms, missed appointments and the rest
That now seemed facile, insignificant
And worth much less than he – or she – had left.

CROSSROADS

Caught at the crossroads with your bike,
I rolled down the window ready
To call your name and make you start
As I drove by that Friday afternoon
But your time came first, the lights changed
And you scooted lamely over to the other side,
Lifted your leg and swung your hip
Before our queue had moved from where it was.

Passing over that junction, I looked left
And saw your back receding as you pushed
Against the breeze and what remained of snow.

I thought then, I might not see you again
So it would make sense to call you up
To settle our account of what we've made
Of life since our last – as you would say –
Discussion, over all the rights and wrongs.

I'd have checked that both of you faired well,
If the girls were back talking to each other
And if you still kept pennies in a tin
For a TV flutter or a hand of cards
That we might yet play on evenings after steaks –
That you'd always take as *well done* as shoe leather
Or send them back to be flame-scorched one more time.

I meant to say, what were you thinking of
But you had passed over and were way out of sight.

BOOTED

Or later, seeing you in the street –
Another winter's day and the pavements crammed
With people half your age or more

About their weekend pleasures – trudging
In your garden boots, buttoned leather jerkin
And a bulging bag – on your way to the bus –

A dew drop hanging from your bulbous nose
And white hairs sprouting from beneath your cap.

I called your name, you sensed it, stopped and turned
Unseeing in a crowd of foreign faces,
Unfamiliar in this place that you'd called home.

Over our glasses of stout, you told me
How the world you knew has changed and left you
Behind bars that sell you nothing that you want

And pleasures you find wanton, lewd and spent.
There is, you said, the racing and a complex
Way of placing bets that limits any loss

Or, when it's warmer still, vegetables
And how you pull them up just to see
They're still alive then watch them till they crop.

I knew you when your body – flexed and firm –
Could master any movement – dab or dart –
When smiling was an art and judgement true.

Before this creeping sickness and the dread,
Before you'd grown accustomed to what's not.

We parted, I took you home and promised
That we'd have another night of cards
One day soon and that I'd be in touch.

VANISHED

You'll be relieved to know
Those hairs that sprouted on your chin –
And caused you so much grief –
Have vanished
And rest now in the hollow
Of your shoulder blade
Along with other remnants of yourself:

The chalk marks on the walls and beams of home –
       rubbed out,
The shadow of a milk churn in the yard –
       forgotten,
Your portrait leaning up against the wall –
       passed down to someone else,
The teapot cooling brown upon the side
       washed and left to dry, turned upside down,
Your apron hanging loose behind the door –
       ripped into dusters to buff a shoe.

Once, celebrating another early spring,
We left behind the beer and barbecue
To find – at last – your modest graveyard lease
And saw that nothing there had changed: the house
In which you were born, lived a life and would have died
Is – taking your short cut across the field – still
Five easy minutes off, if you but had the time.

You'll be surprised to hear of others
That linked us to your past.
They've vanished too
Since you've been gone
And left us here
As current tenants of this place.

Do not concern yourself, strangers have moved
With ease into your vacant space,
Urgent to replace bare bulbs
With recessed lights and stainless steel and taupe –
A colour you would simply have called *Dull,*
In need of a good wipe or a fresh coat.
So, as you'd see, nothing's really vanished here at all
Except the link from you to what here used to be,
Your busy chuckle, stoop and grin
And those ancient bristles sprouting from your chin.

OVER

Dispersed, the afternoon is printed in the grass:
Their voices intermingled with the leaves
Have gone and I am here again

With nothing to achieve or contemplate
And no time left to recollect what was
Or even now what is, or could be,

Or what might have been
Since they left me here that Friday afternoon
Emboldened with the bottle I'd not drink

But which would make them feel that something might
Continue when they'd gone, after the breeze had settled
And they'd tossed that handful that was me into the air –

Watching as the last of what remains gathered,
Drifted and vanished before they
Could hold it in their gaze and let it fall.

There really was – and has been – nothing left
To say or do but to continue – as they have –
Gathering here themselves for rituals and games

That celebrate the something that they share
On days like this until they too will disappear
Like birds and books and bicycles and shoes.

FELINE

The sparrow's disappearing down her throat
Of peristaltic waves and rictus grin
A creature that in goggle-eyed despair
Is watching as its world turns outside in.

And later, luxuriating by the pool,
She stretches out a limb and blithely yawns,
Watching as the hairs rise on her haunch
Whilst scratching at a fragment in the lawn.

She's cast aside the novel in the grass
And wonders now how best she might fulfil
The hours of endless promise – all that choice –
And nothing left except this time to kill.

She cleans a claw and runs a bath of milk
The better to maintain her very best
Until she needs to open up like silk
And rub a leg or – slant-eyed – puff her chest.

This is a world of measured afternoons,
Of languid cigarettes and clotted cream
Where nothing ever happens – never will –
And time itself is nothing but a dream.

She's waiting now to make a final kill,
Another stab at making sense of this
By ending something just to prove she can
Like paring nails or parting with a kiss.

COURGETTES

We measure out the summer in courgettes.
At first – as delicate as fingers – one
And then another, we cut them when they're young –

Children's fingers barely fit to grasp,
We twist their necks and prise them from the bush,
Juice seeping from the wound, they bleed and weep

To be picked and cooked so soon – sealed in oil
As sweet and brief as June, swallowed whole
They leave an aftertaste of burning flesh

Of afternoons and evenings spent outdoors
With so much time to watch another grow
And then another until, in August now,

They're crazed and manic, tumbling out so fast
We cannot stem the flow of great fat limbs
Lolling every dawn, swollen offerings.

The more we pick, the less they'll go to seed,
The more we'll hold the winter back until
The more we've got, there's nothing we can do

To stop them: the fridge becomes a morgue
Of cold and bloated flesh that shines awhile
Then fades and dries – as crisp as death itself.

We have learnt to be inventive, to tame
The rich profusion and the glut: baked tarts,
Strips of pickled flesh, chutneys to preserve

The last of summer and leave a taste to
Savour when the cold has crisped each leaf and
We've had our fill of woody, fly-blown flesh.

We leave each bush to wither and die back.
White leaves and stems so brittle that they snap
When dragged out of the earth and chucked away.

GUNTHORPE

The summer's going fast: wind in the trees
Whose upper boughs are straining as they bounce
And twist against a sky that's leaden grey

The heads of all the flowers have bowed and bent
Towards the grass that's turning green again
Subdued at last – submissive supplicants

We knew it had to end but not like this:
Leaves across a tennis court that's lost its bounce
Rose heads blown and poking swollen hips

Into the wall where yesterday we saw
The last few flowers of clematis – they've gone
Overnight while we were being tossed ourselves

By dreams that rinsed and drained us of the weeks
When we had watched through windows as the sun
Climbed higher until we could imagine

Nothing but another day like this stretching
Into the future – as certain as this
Sad decline from which there will be hours

When we are given back a glimpse of flesh
The puffed décolletage of wrinkled peach –
Late summer's fruit – grown dry and cast aside

The stone adhering in the grass a while
Until it's dried and bleached and buried deep
By leaves – the first of which are falling now

Though most are hanging on despite the breeze –
That's dying back into a sky where clouds
Begin to break and show a petticoat of blue.

AUGUST

Two shoes left empty overnight, pointing
From the seat on which I sat, bone weary
From a day of labour on the plot: dead heading
Roses in the hope that they would come again.
Making sharp the hedges; dredging weeds,
Pulling out the wooded crops and knowing
That everything is going now to seed, is passing
Unto husk and compost, sweet rot and decay.

There's no keeping from this slow decline, this
Torpid gathering of all our broken bits:
Those shards of broken pots piled on the steps,
That pile of wooden spars that were a bench
And yellowed, alopecic grass with weeds
Of shocking green beneath the apple tree.

TERMINAL LOUNGE

We are waiting for something to happen –
It is getting closer to our moment of
Departure, our time approaches – eleven o'clock –
When the busy are about their business
And the young have something better to do.

It's hard to know what can distract us
And keep our minds from the inevitable
In this indifferent place where the drinks are free
And the snacks – we're told – complimentary
Though our time's too short to savour them.

This is the terminal lounge, and we are cut price
Goods in transit about to be shipped
Having completed our terms and tenure.
We know there is no going back and that
Having got this far there is nowhere else to go.

Never having been here before, we don't know
Quite what to do with ourselves; we stand our bags
On end or pile them precariously in aisles.
We will be ready when the moment arrives –
Our eyes stay fixed on the blue revolving screen.

RED SHIFT

This is the lounge of the dispossessed:
Before and after dinner, the pianist
Plays for himself in a vacant space
That fills and empties with the tide.

If there were a crooner, he would croon
And brilliantine his hair between sad tunes.
Instead, the seagulls caulk and scoop
Looking for flotsam on this the longest day.

While he sniffs and snorts his mouthfuls of lamb chop,
Her teeth are clenched – but she's not swallowing
Just chewing on those forty years of bile
As gravy drools and spatters on his chin.

The waiter – solicitous to a fault –
Places a plump hand on her hunched shoulder
And enquires, *Have we both had a good day?*
Which, of course, we have had: *Most certainly.*

Her teeth assay a ripple of delight
But manifest a rictus of decay –
A schoolgirl's coy, coquettish smile
That's laced with mackerel, garlic and pâté

They will all be gone quite soon:
The season turns and when their time is up
Others will shuffle past the boating lake
With time to kill and nothing left to lose.

FOTHERINGHAY

Not so much the last supper as – he might
Have said, clearing his throat – a late lunch
By way of commemoration or even –
Testing the wisdom of his words with a smile –
Commiseration.

There is no castle just a pile of stones.

I regret – she said, fingering her ring –
Nothing, so much as the absence.
And, of course – voiceless – this living death.

      Naturally I
Will be happy to bear the cost myself.

I am, she said, indebted to you but
Allow me to jot one or two things down
Before we go since – as you always said –
Words are not my strongest point.
                Go ahead.
I'll take a walk in the rose garden and
See you down there when you are quite ready.

So – with a flourish laying down the pen,
Readjusting the wig upon her head –
Today, after dinner, I learn my fate.

Mist settles over fields made wet with rain.

They both agree it's best to say:
There's nothing more that really can be said
And place the matter into others' hands.
Misreading this confluence of events,
And right on cue, the attendants arrive
Bearing a flaming torch to celebrate
Another happy anniversary.

Of – she says – my enforced incarceration here.

LIMITED OVERS

It's nearly close of play, the floodlights cast
Their shadows – four by four – across the turf
They've both been here since noon; their sandwiches
Unwrapped, the thermos flask uncorked – they're full

Replete and now it's growing cold and damp.
He's kept the score and she's been knitting rows
Of coloured wool that – fallen on her knee – have made
Alternate stripes of pink and green and white

To make a scarf or cardigan or wrap
Too long to keep a teapot warm – not gloves –
But long enough to last the summer through
And keep from thinking over much about

The season's end – the reckoning – when stumps
Are drawn and they begin the long walk home
Acknowledging some others – stooping too –
Along the way but steadfast in retreat

Behind closed doors until another spring
Will bring them out again – accoutrements intact –
A little less alert but eager to take guard
Until the call of *over* tolls at last.

AND OUT

Nothing can stop the blink of the cursor –
The urgent click of the space bar or the mouse
As the train idles against the platform
Waiting for a signal to drop
Or a light to flash to send us on our way.

Until then we are waiting,
Waiting for the track to be cleared,
After the tape measure has been reeled in,
The crosses made in chalk are photographed
And the labelled pieces placed, in order, in the bag.

We're wondering – looking at our clocks
And sighing for the meeting that we'll miss
Or the over to be bowled that we'll not see –
What has made this happen to us:
Some payback for the wrong that he'd been dealt
Or just the wish to loosen up the vice
And end the sameness of his daily round?
We cannot – and we dare not – know.

But now we're easing forward; the track is clear
And our conscience too is comfortably assuaged:
We'll not be late, there's time enough left now
For coffee and a croissant and a snooze.

The pieces can be neatly rearranged:
As life continues smoothly down the line
We scarcely catch a glimpse as – hurtling through –
They're left to bag the sawdust and hose each other down.

PLATFORM'S EDGE

He's busy watching trains whilst she is not
And now she's back *just checking* he's not strayed
From this his canvas chair that's catching now
The late sun of a summer afternoon

On the platform edge watching as they come
And go; announced, arrived, departed, gone –
It's numbers that he wants: underlined, circled,
Shaded in, the page is incomplete

A catalogue of all that's passed with gaps
That, he hopes, one day to fill but fears he'll not
Since everything that leaves will come again
And those that don't will never pass this way.

She bends her head to his and asks once more:
Have you had enough yet, are you done?
But he is somewhere else – auditing accounts –
Checking lists and totalling each line

To find out what he's missed, what's gone astray
And can't be reckoned or accounted for –
*There's something wrong, this can't be right, I've missed
A trick today – you'll have to give me time.*

And time is all they've got with nothing much
To fill the gaps – but this – in retirement;
One step removed just waiting for a change of trains
The whistle blow before the long ride home.

TUBE

I knew he'd recognised me instantly –
After all those hours we'd spent together
In the past – our eyes met then as now

Momentarily – before he looked away –
Affecting some interest in the news
Or how his jacket bunched about his waist.

So much older; he'd lost a lot of weight
Since the last time; hollowed cheeks, thin hands
And a few last strands of hair across his head.

I'm different too but he knew who I was:
It's in the eyes, they never change – not mine –
I could see my reflection to his right

As we entered the tunnel, left the lights
Behind and rattled deeper underground
Into those past liaisons, those TV evenings

When I pondered if one day I'd be like him
Not thinking that one day I'd face him in the tube
And wonder whether he or I had done

Quite what we'd thought those years ago we would.
Inadmissible evidence that we
Never shared but was always in our minds

Watching each other – cautiously concerned
To keep intact our little illusion
Until the carriage lurched, doors opened, and he left.

LOST

Arriving – two steps at a time –
Urgent and eager at the top of the stairs,
He rests his hand on the banister
And shoots a blank cartridge of wonder
At the space and fix he's in now
Why am I here – what did I come here for?

The memory is blank and the world void
As it stares – clueless – back.

On setting forth, it was all so clear:
The purpose and direction of travel
So precise, the reason and the grasp so
Exact but something that was, got lost
Along the way and turned inside itself
Then disappeared in air.

The pictures on the walls reduced to glass,
He ransacks what remains of memory for a clue.

If only he could retrace each step
And play again those stills of all that's passed –
Frame by every frozen jerky frame –
To relocate the moment when
The great uncertainty began
And he had known precisely what was what.

The loss is only temporary.
He will recover some recognition
Shake his head, smile and carry on –
Until another time when blankness
Leaves him rooted to the spot perplexed
At the sheer opacity of all this
Emptiness from which he came and must as surely go.

SAMHAIN

Frost overnight and the last leaves have
Fallen from the limes whose inky tracings
Are etched against a white sky staining pink
As the sun rises and spills its thin milk

Over the space – transformed – we shared last night;
That outdoor hearth – blanched embers come the dawn –
No longer toasts our inward facing selves
Nor halts the cold from dragging at our backs

What's left – those remnants on the frosted lawn –
Devoid of mystery are simply trash
Consigned to bins and bags and memory
But what remains may last the season out:

A few bright squibs of light, those pumpkin lanterns,
Spumes of singeing sparks that as the flames were dying
Drew us close – clumsily together;
Intimately familiar in the dark

Our faces – half in light – glimpsing one another
Snatching at some scraps of word and song – catching up
Before the long withdrawal unto our own,
Turning our backs on one another once again.

A DIURNAL UPON
ST LUCIE'S DAY

This is the moment of the shortest day,
Lucy, five thirty and I am alone
In the ticking house, alive to no one
And trying to find the words to say,
Simply, how dark it is
And how far from home it seems our centre lies
In all this morning's inky blackness –
Waiting for those squibs of dawn to rise
Again, undone in this godless universe.

At this point, the anchor chain is taut,
As we tug at our moorings the rope strains
And time drips slowly from each plaited strand.
At this precise moment we are caught
Between our wish for home
That old harbour whereto we all must come
And that vertiginous urge to be alone
Gravity free and screaming into space
The glass pressed fast against our hurtling face.

No wonder then that those who came before
Made clamour, walked with candles and lit fires,
Gathered as percussive bands and choirs
And shook this thrumming lodestone to the core
To wring some shreds of light
From the dark shroud of a winter's night
And keep at bay that sempiternal fright
That we are pilot-less and cast adrift
Watching the tide ebb in some far red shift.

The dawn has risen now and given back trees
As outlines etched in ink against a bleached sky.
Radiators and telephones try
To enforce their great illusion and please
Us with their treats once more:
We are beyond the rule of natural law
No longer do we crave a distant shore
The stars have gone, the morning sky is clear
Our pleasures, now, are present and right here.

TEASEL

Ice packed reed beds creak and crack
As the sun eases and releases
Each locked fissure's frosted plate

Close by – etched – teasel teeth – silhouetted –
Sharp barbs – bunched sacrificial heads – shrunk dark
And nodding – firm on stem lengths – eyeless

Husk dry – teased bird beak clean – a mass of them –
Prising each seed head free until the stem
Near breaking, bounces back just as the next one grips

Bloodied beak stem – masked and cowled jet black –
Fifty of them at a count – giving way –
Moving on – wing bars yellow in the sun –

Catching the light as if this were a charm:
Their arrival timed with mine though later –
Doubling back – when I returned – they'd gone

The light had changed – glancing now athwart my eyes –
Towards which – tracking black – some ducks made way
Heading for the remnants of deep midwinter's heat.

DEREK JARMAN'S GARDEN

Another wedding and another chance to buy
The book I've bought them all these twenty years –

Just hoping that by keeping it in print,
The remarrying, the cheerfully gay and

Those who've left it late, might find afterwards
Some comfort in the love he felt for stones,

Rusted coils of spring, frayed ropes and bleached buoys,
Cracked, distressed and peeling strips of wood,

Sea kale, poppies, driftwood held erect,
Daisies, grained and holey pebbles,

Nightshade, valerian, the play of light
On water with skin that's still or ruffled by a breeze,

Studded baths of zinc, faded, damaged, dying things
Brought back to life and busy doing nothing

In the sun – stippled by frost, enlivened
By a shower of rain – unnoticed,

Disregarded and unloved but made proud
And left – in sweet conjunction – to be with

Each other; separate but not apart,
Mindful of the space between that holds them

Balanced, related as they stand yet
Steadfastly alone – and better still for that.

PEBBLES

It would be neat to say, he's doing this
In memory of her: a bed of stones
On which to rest the weight of all those years;

The gleaning of some substance from the grave,
A daily act of penance – in recompense –
For all he might have done and what was left unsaid.

But that would be too pat – an artifice –
For what he's doing now, he's simply on his own –
Quite beached – each day he takes his bucket for a walk

To gather them from gateways, garden plots and streams
These smooth round stones the river rolled before,
Unearthing them, they keep on turning up like dreams:

Russet brown and pink but mostly dun and grey
Occasionally white and pocked with holes
And veined or showing purple in the rain.

He's grading them and says they look their best
When rain has stopped, reflecting slabs of light,
Wedged tight and snug, packed in the wooden box

He's laid – lidless – across that patch of earth
Where nothing ever grew, and no one stopped to look
In shadows for some signs of life – quite dead.

There is still room for a score or more of stones
To cram the edges, finish off the job,
Square things off, step back and lay it all to rest.

TOWARDS BLAKENEY

Incidental as the week itself
The slow uncouplement of time began
To disassociate itself from all
Our certainties and lead us where it would:

Discovering creeks of memory and
How – late afternoon – one single vein
Could slowly burst its narrow banks and bleed
Into the mud until each track had been erased

By the creep of gradual water
That – filling in the space between the reeds –
Reflected back the – early evening – sky
Etched with concentric circles that appeared

Like raindrops falling from an empty sky
As randomly as notes uncast upon a page
Or the bubble of the curlew – at dusk –
Now water had effaced its road of silt.

SALADIN

It took him seventy years to come back
Sucked like time's arrow to the place he started
To find there was no trace of those he'd left behind
Save an envelope and an empty flask gone cold

And his eyes – turned cloudy – could no longer see
No more his brittle ears could hear
As they mouthed their words of welcome –
Confused by his evident distress as

He would have been by them with all their fancy ways
To which he could no longer motion at or mime
To make them understand his deep and present
Thirst for something that they had – anything

That he might recognise of him in them:
A worsted suit, the knotted scarf he'd cast
Across his shoulder or the leather boots
He'd laced and bowed so tight they made him scream.

They lay him on the grass and looked into his eyes
Quite overwhelmed – their breath in clouds
        about his face –
Until his lips began to part and his arms
Fell open – unfolding like a book of psalms

To show what he'd been clutching to his breast
These three score years or more: a lifetime spent
In orbit and descent while his fist had held
A beetle now crusted in a film of ice

Whose eyes like his were open yet but, unlike his,
As jet black as the sun from which they'd come –
Quite deadened by the horror in the skies
That – as they looked – were blinking with surprise.

SESTINA FOR WILLIAM

The Christmas carousel is silent
For once there are no children and you say
Take me for a ride, Grandad, on the horse.
So I do and we circle alone
Catching your mother's all forgiving eye
Laughing as we pass her again and again.

You will never ride the carousel again.
At once discomforted, you fall silent,
Slump your shoulders and narrow your eye
On the hem of your coat so no one might say,
Next time you can ride it all alone.
You can be the rider of your own horse.

Maybe you know that it's the rider not the horse
That goes round and round again and again,
Recycling the cycle steadfastly alone
Knowing that it's best to keep silent
When there's really nothing left to say –
Head against the wall staring with a fixed eye

At a world quite strange, mirrored in your eye.
My grandfather was one who rode a horse
And one who had very little to say
If I asked him to ride me on his knee again
Which I never did since we were bid be silent
To be seen and not heard — always alone —

Learning, as children, to stand alone:
We knew, without demur, to close each eye
At bedtime, mouth our prayers and keep silent
Lest we faltered and fell like a hobbled horse
That would never be able to get up again —
No matter whatever our mothers might say.

So, William, what am I trying to say?
That we all must learn to be alone,
That there is no carousel to get on again,
That you need to see it all with an eye
As patient as a solitary horse
That moves up and down impassive and silent.

Names will come around again, William,
        as often as they say
And though those past are silent; we may still
        not be alone:
So, beware those eyes upon you when you
        ride the fairground horse.

FONTANEL

My palm rests heavy on your head
And I can feel your brain seething
Under – and out of – my grasp
As you spin and weave and knit
The threads together to make some sense
Of what it is that's happening to you.

Asleep now, you are unaware
Of me – as you have always been –
But I am all too aware of you
And your fragility on the brink
Of being – barely remembering to breathe –
Just as likely, I thought, to forget.

I hold my breath and look away
For fear that you will stop altogether.

ACKNOWLEDGEMENTS

THE AUTHOR WOULD like to thank Neil Anderson for his support and encouragement in the compiling of *Dragonflies* and Lorna Brookes for her commitment and attention to detail when editing this book and bringing it safely to print.

ABOUT THE AUTHOR

GRAHAM POWELL has been reading and writing poetry all his life. He draws inspiration from the natural world and the poetry of writers such as Frost, Larkin and Ashbery. He has worked extensively across the education sector and published several books on the nature and purpose of learning. He lives in Cirencester – grows vegetables, walks incessantly and delights in birds, butterflies and dragonflies.

If you loved this book, you'll love these
other poetry collections ...

Brocading the Verse
Julie Wiltshire

*"Memories like autumn leaves blow across my path,
seeking refuge in their own dark space"*

Solitary, beautiful, lyrical ... Julie Wiltshire weaves a tapestry of
loss, grief and redemption in the Cotswold landscape.

ISBN 9781915067272

A Chair at the Café
Hilda Cochrane

Cumbria, Spain, Devon and France ... Hilda Cochrane sets out
on a journey filled with humour and a magical sense of place.
Written on location.

ISBN 9781915067302

Letters from your neighbour far away
Beverley Gordon

A connection is forged between people a world apart.
Insightful, with the originality of a folk tale, this is a
beautiful portrait of a community built by letters, from the
Jhalak Prize nominated author.

ISBN 9781915067081

Crumps Barn Studio
www.crumpsbarnstudio.co.uk